WORLD ALMANAC®

Library of
*American*
GOVERNMENT

# POLITICAL PARTIES,
## INTEREST GROUPS, AND THE MEDIA

BY GEOFFREY M. HORN

**WORLD ALMANAC® LIBRARY**

Please visit our web site at: www.worldalmanaclibrary.com
For a free color catalog describing World Almanac® Library's list
of high-quality books and multimedia programs, call 1-800-848-2928 (USA)
or 1-800-387-3178 (Canada). World Almanac® Library's fax: (414) 332-3567.

Library of Congress Cataloging-in-Publication Data available upon request from publisher.
Fax (414) 336-0157 for the attention of the Publishing Records Department.

ISBN 0-8368-5478-0 (lib. bdg.)
ISBN 0-8368-5483-7 (softcover)

First published in 2004 by
**World Almanac® Library**
330 West Olive Street, Suite 100
Milwaukee, WI 53212 USA

Copyright © 2004 by World Almanac® Library.

Project editor: Alan Wachtel
Project manager: Jonny Brown
Cover design and layout: Melissa Valuch
Photo research: Diane Laska-Swanke
Indexer: Walter Kronenberg
Production: Beth Meinholz

Photo credits: © AP/Wide World Photos: 8, 16, 31 bottom, 35; © Terry Ashe/This Week/Getty Images: 7 bottom;
© Bettmann/CORBIS: 11, 12, 14 both, 15, 21 top, 33, 34, 37 top, 38; © Tyler J. Clements/U.S. Navy/Getty Images:
36; © Karin Cooper/Getty Images: 5; © CORBIS: 9, 20 bottom left; Courtesy National Archives and Records
Administration: cover (background), title page; © Richard Ellis/Getty Images: 40; © Evangelical Environmental
Network/Getty Images: 27; © Najlah Feanny/CORBIS SABA: 28; © Owen Franken/CORBIS: 31 top, 32;
© Douglas Graham/Roll Call/CORBIS SYGMA: 10; © Hulton Archive/Getty Images: 17 top, 19, 20 top, 37 bottom;
© Markowitz Jeffrey/CORBIS SYGMA: 21 bottom; © Catherine Karnow/CORBIS: cover (main); © Brad
Markel/Getty Images: 24 top; © Wally McNamee/CORBIS: 4, 22 bottom, 25, 29; © Eric Miller/Getty Images: 20
bottom right; © Steve Pope/CORBIS SYGMA: 22 top; © Michael Smith/Getty Images: 17 bottom; © Mark
Wilson/Getty Images: 7 top; © Alex Wong/Getty Images: 23, 24 bottom

Printed in the United States of America

1 2 3 4 5 6 7 8 9 07 06 05 04 03

## About the Author

GEOFFREY M. HORN is a freelance writer and editor with a lifelong interest in politics and the arts. He is the author of books for young people and adults, and has contributed hundreds of articles to encyclopedias and other reference books, including *The World Almanac*. He lives in southwestern Virginia, in the foothills of the Blue Ridge Mountains, with his wife, four cats (at last count), and one rambunctious collie. He wishes to thank Bob Famighetti, Mark Sachner, Jonny Brown, Alan Wachtel, and Melissa Valuch for their dedication to this project.

# TABLE OF CONTENTS

Words that appear in the glossary are printed in **boldface** type the first time they occur in the text.

# THE FOURTH BRANCH OF GOVERNMENT

▲ **Members of Congress, the Supreme Court, the executive branch, and the media gathered at the Capitol in 1997 to hear President Bill Clinton deliver his annual State of the Union address.**

Anybody who wants an inside view of American politics and government owes a tremendous debt to Hedrick Smith. In 1988, in the introduction to his book *The Power Game*, Smith recalled how he had come to Washington, D.C., as a young reporter for the *New York Times* more than twenty-five years earlier:

*I thought I understood how Washington worked. I knew the usual textbook precepts that the president and his cabinet were in charge of the government; that Congress declared war and passed budgets; that the secretary of State directed foreign policy. . . .*

Smith soon found out that politics and government were much more complicated than the textbooks suggested:

*Politics in Washington is a continuous contest, a constant scramble for points, for power, and influence. Congress is the principal policy arena of battle, round by round, vote by vote. People there compete, take sides, form teams, and when one action is finished, the teams dissolve, and members form new sides for the next issues. Of course, team competition is our national way of life, but rarely does the contest take place at such close quarters, among people who rub elbows with each other, professionally and socially, day in and day out.*

Washington has changed a great deal since *The Power Game* was written. But Smith's central idea is as true today as it was when Ronald Reagan was president in the 1980s. In order to understand how American government works, you need to understand the roles of Congress, the president, and the Supreme Court. But you also need to know something about the political parties, interest groups, and media outlets that form a major part of the American scene.

⛰ **Reporters are important players on the Washington political scene. Here Defense Secretary Donald Rumsfeld (right) talks to the press in 2001.**

## THREE BRANCHES PLUS ONE

Books about federal power often begin with the idea that the United States government has three branches:
• The legislative branch, headed by Congress, which passes the laws;

## Inside the Beltway

Circling Washington and some of its Maryland and Virginia suburbs is a freeway on which up to 225,000 vehicles drive—or, at peak traffic times, crawl—each working day. The eight-lane road is known as the Capital Beltway or Interstate 495, but most people simply call it "the Beltway."

The Beltway separates Washington and its inner suburbs from the nation that lies beyond. Some commentators in the media, or **pundits**, use the words "inside the Beltway" as a way to show the gap between people in Washington and ordinary Americans. These pundits make the point that Washington has its own unique ways of doing things—ways that people outside politics sometimes find puzzling.

- The executive branch, headed by the president, which carries out the laws; and
- The judicial branch, headed by the Supreme Court, which enforces and interprets the laws.

All this is true—but it is far from the whole truth.

These three branches are the *official* part of the American government. But nothing happens in Washington without the involvement of a fourth branch of government. This *unofficial* branch consists of a small army of media people, political professionals, and **lobbyists** who shape the news we see, the candidates we elect, and the laws Congress passes. Many members of this fourth, unofficial branch work only a mile or two from the White House and the Capitol. No one elects them, and their names are unfamiliar to most Americans. But it is impossible to understand how government really works without understanding who these Washington insiders are and how they operate.

## KEY PLAYERS

The news business is an essential part of the fourth, unofficial branch of government. When Congress cuts taxes, the president sends troops overseas, or the Supreme Court hands down a landmark ruling, the story means big news, and the national news organizations need to cover it. Two of the nation's leading newspapers—the *Washington Post* and *USA Today*—have their headquarters in the Washington area. Great daily newspapers like the *New York Times* and the *Wall Street Journal* maintain offices in the nation's capital. Weekly magazines like *Time* and *Newsweek* also have well-connected Washington staffs.

The major television networks—CBS, NBC, and ABC— and several all-news cable channels assign some of their most experienced reporters to cover events in the nation's

capital. Typically, a major news organization will have different reporters cover Congress, the White House, and the Supreme Court. Other reporters may be asked to cover powerful federal agencies like the departments of Justice and Defense.

Political professionals make up another large part of the fourth branch of government. The two major parties, the Republicans and the Democrats, have their national headquarters in Washington. So do smaller groups like the Libertarian Party and the Green Party. Not all political professionals work directly for political parties, however. Some political pros hire themselves out as **political consultants**, giving advice to candidates on media relations, fund-raising, polling, and policy matters.

More than 20,000 lobbyists in Washington represent the views of many hundreds of special interest groups. Some interest groups side with labor unions, while others support big business.

▲ James Carville (a Democrat) and Mary Matalin (a Republican) are political consultants and pundits as well as husband and wife.

▼ George Stephanopoulos (right) was a top White House aide before becoming a TV political reporter. Here he interviews Senator John Edwards.

Animal rights activists and vegetarians have their own groups. So do cattle farmers and pork producers. Name the topic—abortion, gun rights, cigarette smoking, public aid for private schools—and you'll find interest groups in Washington with sharply opposing viewpoints.

## THE POWER OF ACCESS

Suppose you wanted to make a phone call to the president of the United States. You could pick up the phone and dial the White House switchboard, but unless you had some special connection with the president or the first family, your chances of actually speaking with the president are just about zero. Similarly, you could send a letter or an e-mail to the White House in Washington, D.C., but the likelihood that the president would actually read your message is very small.

There are good reasons why the president would be hard to reach. On any given day, many thousands of people dial the White House switchboard, send the president a letter, or click the e-mail link at the White House home page. No president would ever have time to answer that many messages. Instead, low-ranking staff members handle the large volume of phone, mail, and e-mail traffic.

Relatively few Americans have the chance to talk one-on-one with the president, leading members of Congress, or other top government officials. For this reason, the ability to get very important people to meet with you or answer your phone calls is extremely valuable. In Washington, this is known as the power of **access**. Without access, you have no direct

▼ Dr. Henry Kissinger (left) was secretary of state under President Gerald Ford (right). Since leaving government, Kissinger has headed an influential consulting firm.

## Chambers of Power

Robert Strauss headed Jimmy Carter's winning presidential campaign in 1976, and he served under President Carter and White House chief of staff Hamilton Jordan during the late 1970s. A well-known Democrat, Strauss spoke jokingly with Hedrick Smith in the mid-1980s about the nature of power and access.

▲ **Jimmy Carter, who defeated Gerald Ford in the 1976 presidential election, waves to an enthusiastic crowd.**

*I used to think political power was going to a political dinner. And then I thought political power was helping put on a political dinner. And then I thought it was being invited to stay at the candidate's hotel in a convention city. . . . And then I got to go into the living room of the candidate's suite, and I thought that was something. And then I found out there that the decisions were all made back in the bedroom. And finally, I was invited in the bedroom with the last eight or ten fellas, and then I knew I was on the inside—until I finally learned that they stepped into the john. In the end, just me and Jimmy Carter and Hamilton Jordan made the final decision in the john.*

way to convey your views—or those of the group you represent—to the people who actually make and carry out the laws.

Some people or groups gain access by giving big donations to candidates and political parties. Business and industry groups spend large sums of money to hire Washington lawyers and lobbying firms to present their views to members of Congress and the executive branch. Steps like these are perfectly proper under the First Amendment to the Constitution, which guarantees the right "to petition the Government for a redress of grievances." In simple English, this means people and groups can use every available legal tool to persuade government officials to see things their way.

# Chapter Two

# THE TWO MAJOR PARTIES

▲ Republican supporters of George W. Bush and Democratic backers of Al Gore confront each other after the hotly contested presidential race of 2000.

A political party is a group that seeks to gain power by choosing candidates and getting them elected to public office. To win elections, a party must offer people convincing reasons to choose its candidates over those of the opposition. Since the 1850s, two parties have dominated the American political landscape—the Democratic Party and the Republican Party.

## THE DEMOCRATIC PARTY

The Democratic Party is the oldest political party in the United States. Its roots extend back to the 1790s, when a basic disagreement developed over how much power the federal government should have. People who favored a strong central government were called Federalists. People who wanted the states to have more power were called anti-Federalists.

Over time, the anti-Federalists became known as Democratic-Republicans. Thomas Jefferson, who took office in 1801, was the first Democratic-Republican president. Democrats today still look to him as one of the founders of the Democratic Party.

The Democratic-Republicans splintered in the 1820s. One main faction wanted an activist government that would boost commerce and industry. This faction broke off to become the Whigs, a leading political group from the 1830s to the 1850s. The second main faction favored agriculture, limited government, and states' rights. This second faction is the one that emerged as the modern Democratic Party.

Andrew Jackson, the leader of the Democratic Party, was elected president in 1828. Although the party has changed its stance on many issues since Jackson's day, there is an unbroken historical connection between the Democrats of the late 1820s and Democrats today.

▲ President John F. Kennedy speaking at a 1962 press conference. Decades after his death, he is still a hero to many Democrats.

## "Why I Am a Democrat"

The Democratic National Committee asked visitors to its web site to explain why they supported the Democratic Party. This response came from Gavina Davis of Hayward, California:

*I believe in a clean environment.*

*I believe in the right of every woman to choose and be heard.*

*I believe in the right to vote and that my vote will be counted fairly.*

*I believe in a child's right to a proper education, no matter the social standing of that child.*

*I believe in justice for our senior citizens, a right to decent medical care, affordable medication, and healthy food.*

*I believe in . . . everyone's right to become a member of a union of their choice.*

*I believe in the Democratic way.*

## THE REPUBLICAN PARTY

Although several earlier parties in American history called themselves "Republican," the direct ancestor of today's Republican Party was not established until 1854. The new party arose in response to the problem of slavery.

Slavery had disappeared from the North, but the enslavement of blacks by whites was still the foundation of the southern economy. The crucial question, fiercely debated in the 1850s, was whether slavery should be permitted in the new territories that were organizing on the western frontier. Most white southerners said yes; most northerners said no.

The Democrats had strong roots in the South and did not want to offend the whites who owned slaves. The Whigs had support in both North and South and tried to compromise on the issue. This left an opening for a new party— the Republican Party—that would take a clear stand against the spread of slavery.

In 1861, only seven years after the Republican Party was founded, Abraham Lincoln became the first Republican president. Lincoln led the United States through the worst crisis in the nation's history—the **Civil War**. When the war ended in 1865, the rebellious South had been crushed, the nation had been restored, and slavery had been abolished. Today, at Republican conventions, proud speakers still describe their party as the "party of Lincoln."

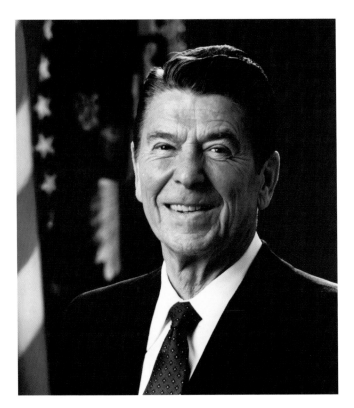

▲ The election of Ronald Reagan as president in 1980 was a triumph for conservative Republicans.

# "Why I Am a Republican"

The Republican Party of Texas—home state of President George W. Bush—asked visitors to its web site to explain why they supported the Republican Party. This answer came from Derrell DeLoach of Pampa, Texas.

*I am a Republican because I believe that people are more capable than the government in creating solutions to the problems faced by them. I also believe [in] decentralized government, low taxes, efficient government spending, law and order, judicial restraint, family values and a strong national defense. As a devoted American, husband, and father of 3 beautiful children, I feel strongly that the Republican Party is committed to a stable future for the American People.*

## THE TWO PARTIES EVOLVE

The Republican Party dominated national politics for more than six decades, winning twelve of the sixteen presidential elections between 1868 and 1928. Outstanding among the Republican leaders during this period was Theodore Roosevelt, who was president from 1901 to 1909. An activist and reformer, TR extended the power of the federal government to crack down on unfair tactics by big companies, preserve the nation's forests and wildlife, and wield a "big stick" in foreign affairs.

The long period of Republican dominance ended with the terrible economic depression of the early 1930s. American voters in 1932 were desperate for change. The president they elected—Franklin D. Roosevelt, or FDR—transformed both the federal government and the Democratic Party. Like TR, his distant cousin, FDR was not bashful about using federal power. His "New Deal" programs built roads and dams, brought electricity to the rural South, provided jobs for millions of people, and offered aid to those in need.

No longer were the Democrats the party of states' rights and limited government. Instead, FDR remade the Democrats into a party that looked not to states, cities, or private companies but to the federal government to solve the nation's problems. A supremely gifted politician, FDR

# Party Animals

In political cartoons, the Democratic Party is often shown as a donkey, while the Republican Party is depicted as an elephant. The donkey image dates back to the presidential election of 1828, when Andrew Jackson's opponents called him a "jackass." Jackson, a Democrat, turned the insult to his benefit by putting the picture of a donkey on his campaign posters.

The first cartoons to make the link between the elephant and the Republican Party were drawn by Thomas Nast in 1874. Nast, the most influential cartoonist of his day, drew Republican voters as an elephant that was easily frightened or fooled.

The Republican Party is sometimes called the GOP—an abbreviation that stands for "Grand Old Party." The term, which began appearing in the 1870s, is somewhat misleading, since the Democratic Party is actually the older of the two major parties.

▷ Thomas Nast depicted the Democratic Party as a donkey in this 1870 political cartoon.

◁ This Nast cartoon dates from 1884, ten years after he had begun using an elephant as a symbol for the GOP.

found support for this approach among a wide variety of groups, including farmers, southern whites, northern blacks, labor union members, immigrants, and **liberals**. By keeping this coalition together, Democrats won seven of nine presidential elections between 1932 and 1964, and kept control of the U.S. House of Representatives for fifty-eight of the sixty-two years from 1933 to 1994.

The New Deal coalition began to weaken in the late 1940s, when northern liberals championed equal rights for black Americans, causing some white southern Democrats to leave the party. Liberal opposition in the 1960s to the **Vietnam War** led to another split among Democrats. Over time, as liberals led the Democratic Party to embrace civil rights, women's rights, abortion rights, and gay rights, **conservatives**—especially religious conservatives—took their votes elsewhere.

Republicans seized the chance to redefine their party. In 1964, Senator Barry Goldwater of Arizona, the leader of the party's conservative wing, became the Republican nominee for president. Although Goldwater lost in a landslide to his Democratic opponent, President Lyndon B. Johnson, the Goldwater campaign attracted many bright young conservative activists to the Republican Party. The conservative Republican surge reached a high-water mark in 1980 with the election of Ronald Reagan as president. Fourteen years later, conservative Republicans broke the Democratic lock on the House of Representatives.

▲ **Conservatives and liberals took different views of civil rights protests in the mid-1960s.**

▲ **Barry Goldwater lost his bid for the presidency in 1964 but drew many conservatives to the Republican Party.**

Today, many Republican leaders continue to view Ronald Reagan as a hero. Reagan, a former Democrat, embraced some of the states'-rights views that Democrats had abandoned. Since Reagan, the Republicans have put traditional family values, strong national defense, support for tax cuts, and opposition to abortion at the center of their agenda.

## Skeptical Views

Some of the nation's best-known writers have been critical of the two-party system. One author, Kurt Vonnegut, Jr., complained that the two parties really cared only about one thing: winning. "When Republicans battle Democrats," he wrote, "this much is certain: Winners will win." The authors of the following excerpts use common stereotypes—for example, the idea that Republicans are the party of the rich, or that Democrats think big government programs can solve any problem—to poke fun at the two major parties and their supporters.

*The Democrats are the party of government activism, the party that says government can make you richer, smarter, taller, and get the chickweed out of your lawn. Republicans are the party that says government doesn't work, and then get elected and prove it.*

—*P. J. O'Rourke*

*The Democrats seem to be basically nicer people, but they have demonstrated time and again that they have the management skills of celery. They're the kind of people who'd stop to help you change a flat, but would somehow manage to set your car on fire. . . . The Republicans, on the other hand, would know how to fix your tire, but they wouldn't bother to stop because they'd want to be on time for Ugly Pants Night at the country club.*

—*Dave Barry*

# THIRD PARTIES

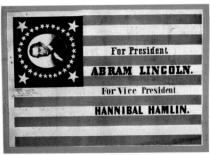

Although Republicans and Democrats have dominated American elections since the Civil War, smaller parties—often called minor parties or "third parties"— have played a notable part in U.S. politics. The Republican Party itself was a "third party" when it was founded in 1854. It successfully contested the dominance of the Democrats and the Whigs, and it became one of the two major parties when the Whigs collapsed.

⬟ When Abraham Lincoln ran for president in 1860, the Republican Party was in its infancy.

Since then, third parties have continued to make an impact on the national political scene. In 1912, for example, Theodore Roosevelt split from the Republicans and ran for president as the candidate of the Progressive (or "Bull Moose") Party. TR's comeback effort did not succeed, but his 1912 campaign brought many of the Progressives' ideas into the political mainstream. Full voting rights for women— endorsed by the Progressives—became the law of the land with the adoption of the Nineteenth Amendment to the U.S. Constitution in 1920. The Progressives also supported social welfare programs to help the ill, the elderly, and the unemployed. These programs became part of Franklin D. Roosevelt's New Deal reforms in the 1930s.

⬟ Campaigning as the presidential candidate of the Green Party, Ralph Nader took many votes away from Democrats in 2000.

In tight contests, third-party candidates have sometimes tipped the balance between the two major-party nominees. A good example of third-party power occurred in the 2000 presidential election, when Ralph Nader, an advocate for consumers' rights, ran as the candidate of the Green Party. Nader captured the votes of many liberals who might otherwise have cast their ballots for the Democratic nominee, Vice President Al Gore. As a result,

Governor George W. Bush of Texas, the Republican candidate, carried just enough states to win the election.

## TROUBLED TIMES, RADICAL RESPONSES

Third parties have often arisen in times of turmoil, when large numbers of Americans felt the two major parties were not dealing with pressing social and economic problems. Some third parties, such as the Progressives, responded to the challenge by promoting fresh ideas and practical reforms. Other groups have pandered to prejudice and resentment.

The Know-Nothings, who had the fastest rise and quickest fall of any third-party movement in U.S. history, were prejudiced against Catholics. The Know-Nothings began in the late 1840s as a series of secret societies with names like the Order of the Sons of America and the Order of the Star Spangled Banner. The movement, which started to call itself the American Party in 1854, was commonly referred to as the Know-Nothings because when members were asked how the party was organized, they were supposed

## Different Voters, Different Choices

In the 2000 presidential election, Al Gore won slightly more than 48 percent of the total vote, while George W. Bush won slightly less than 48 percent. Ralph Nader came in third with a little less than 3 percent, and candidates of all other parties had a combined total of 1 percent. Bush became president because the states he won had more **electoral votes** than those won by Gore.

Opinion polls on Election Day gave a clear view of the differences among those who voted for Bush, Gore, or Nader. Among people who called themselves conservatives, 81 percent voted for Bush, 17 percent for Gore, and 1 percent for Nader. Among people who called themselves liberals, however, only 13 percent chose Bush, while 80 percent voted for Gore, and 6 percent picked Nader.

Race, religion, age, and sexual orientation were clearly linked with voting choices. Gore was the choice of 90 percent of African-American voters, 62 percent of Latinos, 79 percent of Jews, and 70 percent of gays and lesbians. Bush, on the other hand, was preferred by 60 percent of white males and 63 percent of people who attended church more than once a week. Nader drew much of his support from younger voters; he was favored by 5 percent of all voters between the ages of 18 and 29.

to say "I know nothing." The rise of the Know-Nothings came in response to a huge upsurge in immigration to the United States. More than 4 million immigrants landed at American ports between 1840 and 1860. Nearly all of them were from Europe, and a majority of them were Roman Catholics. The Irish left their homeland to escape a terrible famine; many of the immigrants from

▲ **This old print shows Victoria Claflin Woodhull campaigning in 1872. Nominated by the Equal Rights Party, she was the first woman to run for U.S. president.**

Germany and other countries were fleeing political and religious persecution. All these immigrants wanted only to make a better life for themselves and their children. The Know-Nothings, however, saw these newcomers as a threat to the power of the nation's mostly Protestant, English-speaking majority.

By the mid-1850s, the Know-Nothings were the leading party in Massachusetts and had made big gains in other states. Like the Whigs, however, the Know-Nothings fell apart over the issue of slavery. By the end of the decade, the appeal of the Know-Nothings had faded, and the era of Republican dominance was about to begin.

## THIRD PARTIES IN THE MODERN ERA

One of the most consistent—and persistent—American political groups in recent decades has been the Libertarian Party, which was founded in 1971. Libertarians are committed to the idea of personal freedom. "Each individual has the right to control his or her own body, action, speech, and property," says the party's web site. "Government's only role is to help individuals defend themselves from force and fraud." The party is active in all fifty states, and hundreds of its candidates have won local elections, but none of its candidates have ever come close to winning the presidency.

# The Trial of Eugene V. Debs

Eugene V. Debs, a labor leader, was one of the founders of the Socialist Party in 1901. Debs finished fourth in the presidential election of 1912, winning about 6 percent of the popular vote. By that time, about one thousand members of his party had won election to public office in the United States.

Debs, who opposed the U.S. entry into World War I, was arrested in 1918 under a law that made it a crime to oppose the war effort. At his trial he gave a passionate defense of his party's beliefs:

⬆ **Socialist Eugene V. Debs speaking in 1912.**

*I believe, Your Honor, in common with all Socialists, that this nation ought to own and control its own industries. I believe, as all Socialists do, that all things that are jointly needed and used ought to be jointly owned. . . .*

*I am opposing a social order in which it is possible for one man who does absolutely nothing that is useful to amass a fortune of hundreds of millions of dollars, while millions of men and women who work all the days of their lives secure barely enough for a wretched existence.*

While in federal prison, Debs managed to finish third, with more than nine hundred thousand votes, in the presidential election of 1920. Since then, many parties have claimed the name Socialist. Overall support for them has dwindled, in part because these parties have fought bitterly among themselves.

⯈ **1985: Jesse "The Body" Ventura, professional wrestler.**

⯈ **2000: Minnesota governor Jesse Ventura, elected in 1998 on the Reform Party ticket.**

Unlike the Libertarians, most modern third parties have been short-lived and tied to the fortunes of a particular politician. In 1948, for example, Strom Thurmond, the Democratic governor of South Carolina, rebelled against the national Democratic ticket and ran for president as a States' Rights Democrat, or "Dixiecrat." Campaigning as a supporter of racial **segregation**, Thurmond finished third on Election Day. He gained almost all his votes from white southerners who were angry at northern Democrats' support for equal rights for black Americans. Thurmond eventually switched to the Republican Party and set a record as the oldest and longest-serving member in the history of the U.S. Senate.

Another white southerner, George C. Wallace, tapped into the same racial tensions in the late 1960s, when he ran as the presidential candidate of the American Independent Party, winning almost 14 percent of the popular vote. Wallace had become nationally known as a supporter of segregation while he was Democratic governor of Alabama. Law and order, conservative social attitudes, and distrust of the federal government also loomed large in his 1968 campaign. He ran again four years later, this time as a Democrat, but he had to end his campaign when he was shot and badly wounded in Maryland in May 1972.

▲ Governor George Wallace (right) refused to allow African-American students to enter the University of Alabama in 1967. He later ran for president on the American Independent Party ticket.

H. Ross Perot, a business executive, was a thorn in the side of the Democratic and Republican parties during the first half of the 1990s. Perot had a prickly personality, but many voters found his blunt talk refreshing. His key concerns—campaign finance, political corruption, and runaway federal spending—were important issues that the two major political parties had failed to deal with effectively. Running as an independent in 1992, Perot finished a strong third with nearly 20 million votes, the most ever won by a third-party candidate in the United States. Perot launched his own party—the Reform Party—in 1995. By that time, however, his popularity had passed its peak. A struggle for control of the party five years later destroyed the Reform movement as a potent force in national politics.

▼ H. Ross Perot (right) in 1993, with cable talk show host Larry King.

# Chapter Four

# MONEY IN AMERICAN POLITICS

▲ Elizabeth Dole, a Republican, dropped out of the 2000 presidential race because she could not raise enough money.

"Money is the mother's milk of politics," said Jesse Unruh, a California Democrat. What he meant was that, without enough cash, no candidate can win, no matter how intelligent, qualified, likable, and good-looking that candidate may be. To communicate effectively with voters, a candidate needs to advertise, and nearly all forms of advertising—television, radio, newspapers, direct mail, telephone calls, web sites—cost money.

Some candidates have been so hungry for campaign cash that they used questionable fund-raising tactics. When President Bill Clinton was running for reelection in 1996, for example, hundreds of people were invited to visit him at the White House for "coffees" or to stay overnight in the Lincoln Bedroom. Many of these visitors

## With Friends Like These

It's no secret that winners outspend losers in most U.S. political campaigns. But the candidate with the most money does not always come out ahead. In 1995, while running for the Republican presidential nomination, Senator Phil Gramm of Texas told his supporters at a Dallas fund-raising dinner, "Thanks to you, I have the most reliable friend you can have in American politics, and that's ready money." Although Gramm put together a huge campaign treasury, his message fell flat with voters, and he pulled out of the race early in 1996. "When the voter speaks, I listen," he told reporters, "especially when the voter is saying someone else's name."

▲ Senator Phil Gramm in 1994.

had already made large donations to the Democrats or were expected to do so after they met with the president.

## COUNTING THE COSTS

How much money does it take to run for Congress? Information collected by the Federal Election Commission shows that, during the 2001–2002 campaign, each winning candidate in the U.S. House of Representatives raised, on average, about $967,000. To reach this total in only two years—the length of a term in the House—each winning candidate had to raise an average of about $1,325 per day, or about $55 an hour.

While a House candidate has to campaign in a single district, a candidate for the U.S. Senate has the more expensive task of running statewide. To win reelection in an important race in 2002, Senator Mary Landrieu of Louisiana, a Democrat, raised a total of more than $9,750,000. Since a U.S. senator serves a six-year term, that works out to an average of about $4,450 per day. In other words, for every hour of every day of her entire Senate term, she had to raise about $185.

▲ Mary Landrieu (left), a U.S. senator from Louisiana, spent millions of dollars as she successfully fended off a challenge by Suzanne Terrell (right).

Overall, during 2001–2002, the two parties collected more than $1.1 billion. The Republicans raised over $650 million; the Democrats, more than $460 million. The pressure to raise more and more money takes a toll on all Senate and House members. Almost as soon as one campaign ends, the lawmakers need to start raising money for the next one.

## WHERE THE MONEY COMES FROM

Much of the money raised by candidates and political parties comes from private donors. Until recently, no one was

▶ Like many other celebrities, singer Barbra Streisand has used her talents to help political causes.

▼ Two champions of campaign finance reform, Senators John McCain (left) and Russ Feingold (right), pose with citizen activist Doris Haddock, known as "Granny D."

allowed to give more than $1,000 to any particular candidate in any election. This amount was doubled as a result of a law passed in 2002 that limited some of the ways that political parties and interest groups could raise and spend money.

There is no limit to how much of a candidate's own money may be spent on his or her campaign. In 2000, for example, Jon Corzine, a Democrat, spent more than $60 million of his own money to win a U.S. Senate seat from New Jersey. Steve Forbes, a Republican, spent over $75 million of his own money while losing two presidential races, in 1996 and 2000.

For his 2000 presidential campaign, George W. Bush raised about $193 million. Of that total, about $125 million came from private donors. The remaining $68 million came from the Presidential Election Campaign Fund. This federal fund provides money to the major-party presidential candidates and to candidates of third parties that have broad popular support. Money is paid into the fund when individual taxpayers approve a contribution of $3 per person on their annual federal income tax returns.

## POLITICAL ACTION COMMITTEES

When running for Congress, Democrats and Republicans alike rely on funds from **political action committees**, or PACs. PACs raise and spend money to help elect some candidates and defeat others. Labor unions such as the Communications Workers of America have their own PACs.

## The Federal Election Commission

The Federal Election Commission (FEC), an independent government agency, was set up by Congress in 1975 to enforce campaign finance laws and make U.S. elections more honest. Candidates, political parties, and political action committees must file reports telling the FEC how they raised and spent their funds. Much of this information is made public, so voters can know where candidates for president or Congress got their campaign money. The FEC also manages the Presidential Election Campaign Fund.

So do business groups like the National Automobile Dealers Association and professional organizations like the Association of Trial Lawyers of America. All these groups hope the money they contribute will help them gain access and influence.

The first PAC was started in the early 1940s by the Congress of Industrial Organizations, a labor union. This PAC collected small contributions from a large number of union members and used the money to help prolabor candidates. By the 2000 election, there were about 4,500 PACs of all types. They provided about $260 million to candidates for federal office. About 75 percent of that money went to **incumbents**, or current officeholders. The flow of PAC money to incumbents gives them a big advantage over challengers in congressional elections.

▼ **Congressman Newt Gingrich's leadership PAC raised millions of dollars for Republican candidates in the 1990s.**

Some politicians have their own political action committees, called leadership PACs. In 2001–2002, for example, Tom DeLay of Texas, a powerful Republican member of the House of Representatives, gave more than $1 million to other Republican House and Senate candidates. The funds came from his leadership PAC, Americans for a

Republicans Say **YES** To:
- Health Care Reform
- Crime Bill
- Welfare Reform
- Immigration Reform
- Balanced Budget Amendment
- ...s Spending
- FTA
- ...sian Aid
- ...port On Bosnia & Somalia
- ...inet Nominations

Republican Majority. Leadership PACs are a way for politicians who are particularly good at fund-raising to gain and keep influence within their own parties. A candidate who receives money from a leadership PAC will often repay that support by backing the leader on tough votes.

One of the most unusual and successful of all PACs is EMILY's List. This PAC channels money only to female Democratic candidates who support abortion rights and are running for Congress or state governor. EMILY's List was founded in 1985, at a time when relatively few women held high political office. Since then, it has become a main source of funds for female candidates, especially women of color, who might otherwise have a hard time raising enough money to run effective campaigns. The PAC—whose name stands for "Early Money Is Like Yeast"—prides itself on giving money early, so each favored candidate can get a quick start.

## Cattle Calls

One way for members of Congress to raise money for their campaigns is to hold fund-raising events and invite representatives of fifty to one hundred PACs. The system was described by James Rogan, a Republican who represented a southern California district in Congress in the late 1990s. Rogan spoke with an interviewer from the Center for Responsive Politics, a clean-government group.

The truth is, from a member's perspective we call them cattle calls. You stand there for an hour and a half and you have people eating finger food, all walking by saying "Hi, I'm Joe Johnson from Independent Meat Packers Association, I'm just glad to be here," and off they go.

And the scary thing is that I could shake those hands on Monday night, and I could trip over them on Wednesday and not recognize them. I was always worried that they could give $1,000 to my campaign on Monday night and I could shake their hand, and walk past them in the Capitol on Wednesday night and not acknowledge them because I don't remember them, and have them say what a jerk Rogan is. So I just found that when someone would smile at me I would just smile back because I didn't know if they were a . . . donor or someone else that was helping me and I just didn't remember them.

The truth is that there are so many folks in town, and unless you've been here a for a really long time, and you've worked with people, they're just faces in the crowd.

# INTEREST GROUPS AND LOBBYISTS

# Chapter Five

You won't find it highlighted on most tourist maps, but no place in Washington is more central to the way government really works than K Street, which is located a few blocks north of the White House and the Capitol. K Street is the center of the lobbying industry. Here and elsewhere in the nation's capital, more than 20,000 lobbyists represent many hundreds of interest groups. These lobbyists—who, unlike members of Congress, are not elected by the voters—weigh in on just about every measure that Congress considers and the executive branch carries out.

To some, the question might seem amusing. But we take it seriously. As our Savior and Lord Jesus Christ teaches us, "Love your neighbor as yourself." (Mk 12:30-31)

Of all the choices we make as consumers, the cars we drive have the single biggest impact on all of God's creation.

Car pollution causes illness and death, and most afflicts the elderly, poor, sick and young. It also contributes to global warming, putting millions at risk from drought, flood, hunger and homelessness.

Transportation is now a moral choice and an issue for Christian reflection. It's about more than engineering—it's about ethics. About obedience. About loving our neighbor.

So what *would* Jesus drive?

We call upon America's automobile industry to manufacture more fuel-efficient vehicles. And we call upon Christians to drive them.

Because it's about more than vehicles—it's about values.

Rev. Clive Calver, Ph.D.
President, World Relief
Rev. Richard Cizik
Vice President for Governmental Affairs, National Association of Evangelicals
Loren Cunningham
Founder, Youth with a Mission
President, University of the Nations

Rev. David H. Englehard, Ph.D.
General Secretary, Christian Reformed Church in North America
Millard Fuller
Founder & President, Habitat for Humanity International
Rev. Vernon Grounds, Ph.D.
Chancellor, Denver Seminary

Rev. Steve Hayner, Ph.D.
Past President, InterVarsity Christian Fellowship
Rev. Roberta Hestenes, Ph.D.
International Minister, World Vision
Rev. Richard Mouw, Ph.D.
President, Fuller Theological Seminary
Rev. Ron Sider, Ph.D.
President, Evangelicals for Social Action

Sponsored By THE EVANGELICAL ENVIRONMENTAL NETWORK
10 East Lancaster Ave., Wynnewood, PA 19096 www.WhatWouldJesusDrive.org
Partial list of signatories. Affiliations listed for identification only.

▲ **Special interest groups sometimes promote their views through advertising. This magazine and TV ad campaign ran in 2002.**

## WHAT LOBBYISTS DO

The term "lobbyist" is based on the common English word "lobby," meaning an entrance hall, corridor, or waiting room. The political use of the term comes from England, where, centuries ago, private citizens would directly promote their interests to members of Parliament in the halls of the House of Commons. Today, interest groups are often called "lobbies," and the people paid to represent these groups are known as lobbyists.

Some of the most effective lobbyists are former federal officeholders, including former Senate and House members and former top congressional staffers. More than one hundred former members

### State Lobbies

Lobbyists operate not only in Washington but also in the fifty state capitals, where the state legislatures meet. By the end of the 1990s, about 45,000 lobbyists were registered with state legislatures.

of Congress work as lobbyists. Many former members of executive branch agencies now lobby on behalf of the industries they used to regulate. To slow down the "revolving door" between federal government agencies and interest groups, laws and ethics rules require people who leave federal office to wait a year or more before they can lobby the agencies where they worked. Paid lobbyists must register and file financial forms with the House and the Senate.

Lobbies work in different ways. The most important behind-the-scenes job lobbyists do is to supply lawmakers and other officeholders with up-to-date information. For example, before deciding whether to vote money to build more airports, a member of Congress might want to talk both with lobbyists for the airline industry and with lobbyists for consumer groups to see whether the new airports are needed.

Interest groups sometimes take a much more visible role. In 1993–1994, for example, the Health Insurance Association of America spent millions of dollars on a series of TV ads featuring a fictional couple, Harry and Louise. The ads opposed a new federal health care program submitted to Congress by President Bill Clinton. The private health insurance firms represented by the association saw the Clinton plan as a threat to their interests, and were delighted when the "Harry and Louise" ads helped to kill it.

▲ **Members of the New York Hotel Trades Council Pensioners Society express their views on health care reform in 1993.**

Lobbyists actually write or revise many bills, and work within Congress to weaken or bury the measures they oppose. Because many bills that come before Congress are very long and complicated, members of the House and Senate cannot study

## A Lobbyist Takes on Congress

Lobbyists make their living dealing with politicians, but not all lobbyists are happy about how the system works. Here is what Wright Andrews, a former president of the American League of Lobbyists, said about Congress in an interview in 2002:

> *I find the quality of legislators in going down because the members today have to spend so darn much time raising money they don't get to spend nearly adequate amounts of time focusing on the finer points of legislation. Do you realize that almost all the bills that are passed in the Congress, and voted on, have not been read by the members that voted on them? . . . Almost none of them! Any member that was honest will tell you that. They don't go through things in great detail. They don't have the time. That's the problem with the fund-raising system.*

every part of every measure they vote on. Especially in the hurried days at the end of a session, when members are preparing to leave town, lobbyists can use their access to congressional leaders to tack on provisions that benefit special interests. A measure with many such provisions is sometimes called a "Christmas tree bill."

▼ **People for the Ethical Treatment of Animals (PETA) is an interest group that promotes the idea of animal rights.**

### LEADING INTEREST GROUPS

Interest groups wield political power through their lobbying efforts, political action committees (PACs), or grassroots organizing skills—and, sometimes, through a combination of all three. In general, labor unions, lawyers' associations, environmental groups, and the entertainment industry support the Democratic Party. Prominent supporters of the Republican Party include defense-related industries, banking and insurance firms, energy companies, and the health and transportation sectors.

## What Is a "Think Tank"?

Before the federal government can take action to deal with a difficult problem, lawmakers and planners need to know what the possible solutions are, how much each will cost, and how effective each might be. To find answers to questions like these, government officials turn to experts and scholars outside government. Some of these experts work in "think tanks"—interest groups that do research and recommend ideas that government officials then put into practice. Washington has many think tanks, representing many different points of view.

Between 1989 and 2002, members and PACs connected with one labor union, the American Federation of State, County and Municipal Employees, contributed more than $33 million, almost all of it to Democrats. Unions have also been the backbone of Democratic get-out-the-vote efforts on Election Day. Individuals and PACs connected with Philip Morris, the world's number-one tobacco firm, donated more than $19 million to political parties and candidates from 1989 through 2002. The company, which changed its name to the Altria Group in 2003, gave about 75 percent of that total to Republicans.

Other important interest groups include:

• **American Association of Retired Persons (AARP):** Founded in 1958. Represents more than 35 million members, all of them at least fifty years old. Influential on Social Security, health care, and other issues of particular concern to the elderly.

• **American Israel Public Affairs Committee (AIPAC):** Founded in 1954. Promotes economic aid and military support for the State of Israel. Keeps a low public profile but remains one of Washington's most formidable lobbies.

• **Christian Coalition:** Founded in 1989. Describes itself as "the largest and most active conservative grassroots political organization in America." Strongly antiabortion. Although officially **nonpartisan**, the Christian Coalition represents a core group of Republican supporters among religious conservatives.

• **National Organization for Women (NOW):** Founded in 1966. The nation's best-known women's rights group. Strongly in favor of abortion rights. Although officially nonpartisan, NOW represents a core group of Democratic supporters among liberal women.

⛰ Members and supporters of NOW at a pro-choice rally in 1992.

• **National Rifle Association (NRA):** Founded in 1871. Uncompromising defender of gun rights and opponent of gun control. Ranked by *Fortune* magazine as the most powerful of all lobbying groups in 2002. More than 80 percent of its campaign donations support Republican candidates.

◀ Actor Charlton Heston (left) led the National Rifle Association from 1998 to 2003. Next to him is the NRA's executive vice president, Wayne LaPierre.

# Chapter Six

# PRESS AND POLITICS

▲ **Investigations of the Watergate scandal by newspaper reporters and others led to President Nixon's resignation in 1974.**

Politicians have a love-hate relationship with the press, which has the power to make or break their political careers. Presidents like Theodore Roosevelt, Franklin D. Roosevelt, John F. Kennedy, and Ronald Reagan made expert use of the media in order to boost their own popularity and win support for their programs. On the other hand, damaging news reports helped to end the presidency of Richard Nixon and have sunk many candidates' election hopes.

## GETTING THE NEWS

Americans get the news from a wide variety of sources. Newspapers were the dominant news source through the end of the nineteenth century. Radio entered the mix as a news medium in the 1920s, broadcast television in the late 1940s, cable television in the early 1980s, and the Internet in the mid-1990s.

Today, many Americans follow the news on TV and computer screens rather than in print. Nevertheless, daily newspapers and weekly magazines still hold an important place on the Washington political scene. The United States has more than fourteen hundred daily newspapers. The total number of copies printed each day is around 55 million—about one for every five Americans.

Most newspapers try to separate the news, which is reported on the news pages, from opinion, which is offered on the editorial pages. Good reporters make an effort to present the news in a way that is factual, accurate, balanced, and fair. Editorial writers, on the other hand, mix fact with opinion in order to persuade their readers to embrace a particular point of view. Writers for magazines like the liberal *Nation* or the conservative *National Review* also mix fact with opinion in ways that clearly reflect each magazine's political viewpoint.

▲ **William F. Buckley, Jr., founded the conservative** *National Review* **in 1955, three years before this picture was taken.**

## GROWTH OF NEWSPAPERS

Freedom of the press is fundamental to the U.S. system of government. The First Amendment to the Constitution—part of the Bill of Rights—provides that "Congress shall make no law . . . abridging the freedom of speech, or of the press."

The federal government has, at times, tried to censor the press, but such lapses have been unpopular and relatively brief. In 1798, for example, Congress passed several measures known as the Alien and Sedition Acts. These laws imposed stiff penalties on newspapers that published "any false, scandalous and malicious writing" about the president, the federal government, or either house of Congress. The laws were, at heart, an attempt by the Federalists, who controlled the government, to stifle criticism from their Democratic-Republican opponents (see Chapter 2). The public responded by voting the Federalists out of office and electing Democratic-Republican candidates instead.

The publishing of newspapers and pamphlets in the young nation was largely allied with or controlled by political parties. In the 1830s, however, came the birth

▲ A political cartoonist in 1895 depicted President William McKinley trying to silence so-called "yellow" journalists. He was concerned that their biased reporting would turn public opinion against his policies.

of the "penny press"—cheap, mass-produced papers that expanded the idea of news to include lurid crime tales and other attention-getting features. Seeking to attract more and more readers, many newspapers at the end of the nineteenth century relied on big, bold headlines, sensational stories, patriotic appeals, and novelties such as comic strips. News reports in these papers emphasized rumor and exaggeration rather than fact—a trend known as "yellow journalism." This kind of journalism lives on in some of the **tabloids** displayed at check-out lanes and on racks at supermarkets and convenience stores.

American newspapers have long taken pride in exposing corruption by government officials. A high point in U.S. newspaper history came in the early 1970s, when two young reporters for the *Washington Post*, Bob Woodward and Carl Bernstein, exposed the Watergate scandal. The scandal began on June 17, 1972, when five burglars were arrested

## The Associated Press

The invention of the telegraph in 1837 made it possible for news to travel from one city to another in a matter of minutes. In 1848, six New York City newspapers agreed to share the costs of transmitting news reports by telegraph wire. The result was the first "wire service"—the Associated Press.

Over the decades, as the telegraph has been replaced by the telephone and the Internet, the Associated Press has grown to become the world's largest news organization. The AP maintains more than 240 bureaus in cities around the globe. It supplies news and photos to over fifteen thousand TV and radio stations and newspapers worldwide, reaching an audience of more than one billion people each day. The AP's coverage of U.S. politics is especially important for the many newspapers that cannot afford to send their own reporters to Washington.

## Feeding Frenzy

When a top political figure becomes the subject of scandal, dozens of reporters for the major daily newspapers and television networks may all begin working on the story at the same time. Hour by hour, day by day, as new scraps of information emerge, TV mobile units keep watch outside the politician's home, and reporters camp on the family's front lawn.

This kind of behavior is sometimes called a feeding frenzy. The term comes from the behavior of sharks, who are said to grow increasingly excited as they circle their wounded prey. An example of a feeding frenzy took place in May 1987, after one newspaper revealed that Gary Hart, a Democratic presidential candidate, was dating an attractive young woman in Florida while his wife was at home in Colorado. In less than a week, Hart was forced to drop out of the presidential race.

▲ **The press swarmed around the White House in 1998 during a sex scandal involving President Clinton.**

while trying to break into Democratic National Committee headquarters in Washington, D.C. President Nixon, a Republican, feared that a full investigation of the burglary would uncover improper and illegal actions by members of his staff. Taped conversations between Nixon and his top aides reveal that he approved payoffs to the burglars, in order to buy their silence, and that he tried to get government agencies to cooperate in covering up the crime. The *Washington Post* articles and those by other reporters helped to unravel the cover-up and led to Nixon's resignation from the presidency in August 1974.

## POLITICIANS AND REPORTERS

Political leaders need the media in order to communicate with voters and shape debates over public policy. Some politicians hold regular press conferences, at which they answer questions from groups of journalists. Others may grant one-on-one interviews with favored reporters. Newspapers and magazines that run positive stories about a particular politician may be rewarded with additional access. That same politician may punish reporters who write unhelpful stories by refusing to answer their phone calls.

▲ President George W. Bush gave the thumbs-up sign to reporters, officers, and sailors on the deck of the USS *Abraham Lincoln*, where he announced that major combat in the Iraq war was over.

One of the most controversial ways of communicating with the public is through "leaks." Leaking involves the release of secret, sensitive, or embarrassing information, often in exchange for a reporter's promise not to reveal the source's name. Some leaks are intended to expose wrongdoing; for example, an employee might leak information about a supervisor who is incompetent or corrupt. Other leaks—called "trial balloons"— may be quietly launched by politicians and their aides in order to test support for a particular idea or program. If the idea is a dud, the source who launched the trial balloon avoids public criticism. If the trial balloon gets a good reception, the officeholder can later claim credit when the proposal is made officially.

A gifted politician will always seek to manage the news to get the best possible press coverage. For example, after U.S. armed forces toppled the government of Iraq in April 2003, President Bush underlined his role as commander in chief by landing on the deck of the aircraft carrier *Abraham Lincoln* and making a dramatic speech. Michael Deaver, a longtime aide to Ronald Reagan, was a master at placing the president in splendid settings that played especially well on newspaper front pages and TV newscasts.

# Chapter Seven

# ELECTRONIC MEDIA

The electronic media have come a long way since President Franklin D. Roosevelt gave his first radio talk, or "fireside chat," in 1933. Today, radio, television, and the Internet are the main means by which people inside the Beltway connect with the outside world—and, increasingly, the way that political activists far from Washington connect with each other.

## RADIO AND NETWORK TELEVISION

According to a recent survey by the Pew Research Center for the People and the Press, about two of every five adults in the United States continue to rely on radio as a source for news. Conservative talk-show hosts such as Rush Limbaugh have millions of regular listeners, many of whom vote Republican on Election Day.

In the early 1990s, about 60 percent of adult Americans watched the nightly news on the three major broadcast networks—CBS, NBC, and ABC. Ten years later, the network news audience had dropped by half. Viewers continued to turn to network television for major events, however, such as the president's annual State of the Union address to Congress, televised debates between the major-party candidates for president, and reports on national crises such as the terrorist attacks against the United States on September 11, 2001.

▲ President Franklin D. Roosevelt delivering one of his radio "fireside chats."

▼ Barbara Walters moved from NBC's "Today Show" to ABC in 1976, becoming the first woman to cohost a nightly TV network newscast.

## ¡Noticiero en español!

If you understood the headline ("Newscast in Spanish!"), you may already know that Spanish-language broadcasting is an increasingly important part of the U.S. media mix. More than 38 million Latinos live in the United States. They make up a large group of voters in key states like California, Texas, New York, Florida, and Illinois, and politicians have been trying hard to reach them through both English- and Spanish-language programming. Univision is the nation's largest Spanish-language broadcaster and one of the fastest-growing media companies in the United States.

▲ **Henry Cisneros, a prominent Latino, has held top positions in politics and broadcasting.**

Television also communicates information in other ways. A surprising number of people get their political news from late-night entertainers such as Jay Leno and David Letterman or from the long-running comedy program *Saturday Night Live*. A much smaller but politically savvy audience tunes to Sunday morning TV talk shows and interview programs.

### CABLE AND THE INTERNET

As fewer Americans click on CBS, NBC, and ABC for the nightly news, more viewers have turned to cable news channels. About one-third of adult Americans watch cable news regularly. The first all-news cable channel—the Cable News Network, or CNN—was founded in 1980. Although CNN has a huge worldwide presence, it faces tough competition for U.S. viewers from the Fox News Channel and from MSNBC and CNBC, two cable news operations within the NBC family.

A news organization with a smaller but very loyal audience is C-SPAN, or the Cable-Satellite Public Affairs

Network. C-SPAN provides daily coverage of the Senate and House of Representatives, and presents round-the-clock public affairs programming on TV, radio, and the World Wide Web.

In the mid-1990s, only 2 percent of U.S. adults regularly turned to the Internet for news; today, that figure exceeds 25 percent. Just about every broadcast or cable network has a presence on the World Wide Web. The web has also become an indispensable tool for presidential candidates, who use the Internet to attract and inform voters and to raise campaign funds.

## MEDIA AND THE FUTURE

Successful politicians adjust. Just as earlier officeholders mastered radio and TV, today's political leaders will need to use the new media effectively if they wish to serve the public and keep their jobs.

One problem posed by the cable news channels is that of nonstop coverage. Fifty years ago, the cycle of news reporting was much simpler: newspapers published once or twice a day, and each TV network produced a fifteen-minute newscast every evening. Today, politicians must cater to cable channels that operate twenty-four hours a day, seven days a week, 365 days a year. They must be ready to respond to major events or answer an opponent's accusations at any hour of the day or night.

A second problem for political professionals is the development of "narrowcasting." Three decades ago, top government officials could reach the bulk of the American audience through the three major networks. Today, however, there are hundreds of cable channels and a bewildering variety of other outlets. To send the right message to the right audience requires highly skilled media consultants.

Some media critics worry about the fact that a large number of TV and radio stations, cable channels, newspapers, magazines, Internet content providers, and entertainment firms are controlled by a handful of very large companies, such as Disney and AOL Time Warner. These critics fear that this concentration of media power may make it difficult for independent voices to be heard.

One possible answer to control of the media by a few large companies is the growing use of the Internet by ordinary citizens. In early 2003, as the nation's political leaders and news networks geared up for war in Iraq, activists for the first time employed e-mail to organize large-scale antiwar protests. Use of the Internet as a tool for citizen action by people of all political views is one of the most exciting ways the new electronic media may transform American government.

## Birth of the Blogs

**Blog** is short for weblog—a kind of online diary that contains clickable links to other blogs and to Internet news sites. A growing number of pundits, both amateurs and professionals, have their own blogs. Reporters traveling with U.S. and British troops in Iraq during March and April 2003 used their laptop computers to post "warblogs" from the battlefront.

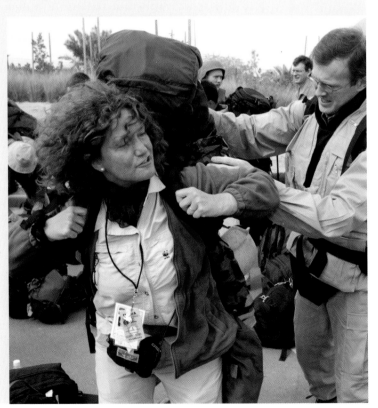

In 2003, hundreds of journalists "embedded" with U.S. troops covered the Iraq war from the front lines.

# POPULAR VOTE FOR PRESIDENT, BY CANDIDATES AND PARTIES (2000)

| Candidate (Party Label) | Popular Vote Total | Share of Popular Vote (%) |
|---|---|---|
| Al Gore (Democrat) | 50,999,897 | 48.38 |
| George W. Bush (Republican) | 50,456,002 | 47.87 |
| Ralph Nader (Green) | 2,882,955 | 2.74 |
| Patrick J. Buchanan (Reform/Independent) | 448,895 | 0.42 |
| Harry Browne (Libertarian) | 384,431 | 0.36 |
| Howard Phillips (Constitution) | 98,020 | 0.09 |
| John S. Hagelin (Natural Law/Reform/Indep.) | 83,714 | 0.08 |
| Write-In (Misc.) | 20,767* | 0.02 |
| James E. Harris, Jr. (Socialist Workers) | 7,378 | 0.01 |
| L. Neil Smith (Libertarian) | 5,775 | 0.00 |
| David McReynolds (Socialist) | 5,602 | 0.00 |
| Monica Moorehead (Workers World) | 4,795 | 0.00 |
| None of These Candidates (Nevada) | 3,315 | 0.00 |
| Cathy Gordon Brown (Independent) | 1,606 | 0.00 |
| Denny Lane (Vermont Grassroots) | 1,044 | 0.00 |
| Randall Venson (Independent) | 535 | 0.00 |
| Earl F. Dodge (Prohibition) | 208 | 0.00 |
| Louie G. Youngkeit (Independent) | 161 | 0.00 |
| **Total:** | 105,405,100* | |

**Voting age population (Census Bureau Population Survey for November 2000): 205,815,000
Percentage of voting age population casting a vote for president: 51.21%**

Notes: Includes all candidates listed on at least one state ballot. Party designations vary from one state to another. Vote totals for the candidates listed above include any write-in votes they received.

*Totals do not include the 138,216 miscellaneous write-in, blank, and void votes that were compiled as one total in New York.

*SOURCE: Federal Election Commission*

## CONTRIBUTIONS TO CONGRESSIONAL CANDIDATES, RANKED BY INDUSTRY

| Rank | Industry | Total | To Democrats | To Republicans |
|------|----------|-------|--------------|----------------|
| 1 | Lawyers/Law Firms | $36,342,243 | 69% | 31% |
| 2 | Retired | $21,632,287 | 43% | 56% |
| 3 | Health Professionals | $21,339,901 | 44% | 56% |
| 4 | Real Estate | $18,535,084 | 52% | 48% |
| 5 | Securities/Invest | $15,572,035 | 56% | 44% |
| 6 | Insurance | $14,303,166 | 39% | 60% |
| 7 | Leadership PACs | $12,810,899 | 40% | 60% |
| 8 | Commercial Banks | $10,449,141 | 41% | 59% |
| 9 | Transport Unions | $10,135,714 | 81% | 19% |
| 10 | Electric Utilities | $9,911,441 | 40% | 60% |
| 11 | Public Sector Unions | $9,092,787 | 85% | 15% |
| 12 | Lobbyists | $8,977,553 | 52% | 48% |
| 13 | Bldg Trade Unions | $8,560,157 | 84% | 15% |
| 14 | Oil & Gas | $8,226,107 | 28% | 72% |
| 15 | Business Services | $7,756,378 | 53% | 46% |
| 16 | Industrial Unions | $7,632,831 | 97% | 2% |
| 17 | Pharm/Health Prod | $7,579,083 | 35% | 65% |
| 18 | TV/Movies/Music | $7,097,477 | 62% | 38% |
| 19 | General Contractors | $6,927,492 | 33% | 67% |
| 20 | Automotive | $6,749,667 | 33% | 67% |

SOURCE: Center for Responsive Politics, based on data from the Federal Election Commission. All data are for the 2001–2002 election cycle.

# MAJOR U.S DAILY NEWSPAPERS, RANKED BY CIRCULATION

| Rank | Newspaper | Average Daily Circulation |
|---|---|---|
| 1 | Arlington (VA) USA Today (m) | 2,149,933 |
| 2 | New York (NY) Wall Street Journal (m) | 1,780,605 |
| 3 | New York (NY) Times (m) | 1,109,371 |
| 4 | Los Angeles (CA) Times (m) | 944,303 |
| 5 | Washington (DC) Post (m) | 759,864 |
| 6 | New York (NY) Daily News (m) | 734,473 |
| 7 | Chicago (IL) Tribune (m) | 675,847 |
| 8 | Long Island (NY) Newsday (m) | 577,354 |
| 9 | Houston (TX) Chronicle (m) | 551,854 |
| 10 | New York (NY) Post (m) | 533,860 |
| 11 | San Francisco (CA) Chronicle (a) | 512,042 |
| 12 | Dallas (TX) Morning News (m) | 494,890 |
| 13 | Chicago (IL) Sun-Times (m) | 480,920 |
| 14 | Boston (MA) Globe (m) | 471,199 |
| 15 | Phoenix (AZ) Arizona Republic (m) | 451,288 |
| 16 | Newark (NJ) Star-Ledger (m) | 410,547 |
| 17 | Atlanta (GA) Journal-Constitution (m) | 396,464 |
| 18 | Detroit (MI) Free Press (m) | 371,261 |
| 19 | Philadelphia (PA) Inquirer (m) | 365,154 |
| 20 | Cleveland (OH) Plain Dealer (m) | 359,978 |
| 21 | San Diego (CA) Union-Tribune (m) | 351,762 |
| 22 | Portland (OR) Oregonian (a) | 351,303 |
| 23 | Minneapolis (MN) Star Tribune (m) | 340,445 |
| 24 | Saint Petersburg (FL) Times (m) | 331,903 |
| 25 | Orange County (CA) Register (m) | 324,056 |
| 26 | Miami (FL) Herald (m) | 317,690 |
| 27 | Denver (CO) Rocky Mountain News (m) | 309,938 |
| 28 | Baltimore (MD) Sun (m) | 306,341 |
| 29 | Denver (CO) Post (m) | 305,929 |
| 30 | Saint Louis (MO) Post-Dispatch (m) | 290,615 |

Notes: All data as of September 30, 2001.
(m) = morning    (a) = afternoon

*SOURCE: Editor and Publisher International Yearbook.*

# TIME LINE

| | |
|---|---|
| **1796** | First U.S. presidential election in which political parties, or "factions," play a role. |
| **1798** | Congress passes Alien and Sedition Acts. |
| **1828** | Andrew Jackson leads the Democratic Party to victory in the presidential election. |
| **1848** | Associated Press news agency founded. |
| **1854** | Republican Party established. |
| **1861-65** | Civil War. |
| **1901** | Socialist Party founded. |
| **1912** | Theodore Roosevelt splits the Republican Party, running for president on Progressive ("Bull Moose") ticket. |
| **1932** | Franklin D. Roosevelt wins the first of his four presidential elections, building Democrats' "New Deal" coalition. |
| **1948** | Resistance to civil rights leads "Dixiecrats" to break from the Democratic Party. |
| **1964** | Barry Goldwater remakes the Republican Party is his own conservative image during his losing presidential campaign. |
| **1968** | George Wallace wins almost 14 percent of the popular vote as presidential candidate of the American Independent Party. |
| **1971** | Libertarian Party founded. |
| **1972** | *Washington Post* reporters uncover Watergate scandal. |
| **1975** | Federal Election Commission established. |
| **1980** | Ronald Reagan, a conservative Republican, wins the presidential election. |
| **1992** | Businessman H. Ross Perot mounts a strong third-party challenge to Bill Clinton and George H. W. Bush. |
| **1994** | Republicans win majority in the House of Representatives for the first time in four decades. |
| **2000** | Green Party nominee Ralph Nader finishes third in the popular vote for president behind Al Gore and George W. Bush. |
| **2002** | Congressional elections leave Republicans in control of the presidency, Senate, and House of Representatives. |

# GLOSSARY

**access:** the power to get very important people to meet with you or answer your phone calls.

**blog:** short for "weblog"; an online diary that contains links to other blogs and Internet news sites.

**Civil War:** a war (1861–1865) between northern and southern states that began when the South rebelled against the Union. Slavery in the South was a major cause of the conflict, which was won by the North.

**conservatives:** people who favor traditional views and values, while working to slow the pace of social change.

**electoral votes:** the votes cast by each state in choosing the president, equal to the number of that state's members of the U.S. Senate and House of Representatives.

**incumbents:** current officeholders.

**liberals:** people who support political, economic, and social reforms and tend to favor new ideas over traditional views and values.

**lobbyists:** people hired by special interest groups to influence the decisions of members of Congress or other public officials.

**nonpartisan:** not officially connected with any political party.

**political action committees (PACs):** groups that raise and spend money to help elect some candidates and defeat others.

**political consultants:** experts who earn their living by advising candidates for public office.

**pundits:** commentators in the media.

**segregation:** separation of one racial group from another, enforced by law.

**tabloids:** newspapers that are narrower than a standard-sized newspaper and often feature sensational headlines and lurid stories.

**Vietnam War:** a war fought by the United States in Southeast Asia mainly from the mid-1960s through the early 1970s.

**World War I:** a war fought mainly in Europe during 1914–1918. The United States entered the war in 1917, siding with England and France against Germany and Austria-Hungary.

# TO FIND OUT MORE

## BOOKS

Bibby, John F., and L. Sandy Maisel.
***Two Parties—Or More? The
American Party System.***
Boulder: Westview Press, 2002.

Fish, Bruce, and Becky Durost Fish.
***The History of the Democratic
Party.***
Philadelphia: Chelsea House, 2000.

Lutz, Norma Jean.
***The History of the Republican
Party.***
Philadelphia: Chelsea House, 2000.

Lutz, Norma Jean.
***The History of Third Parties.***
Philadelphia: Chelsea House, 2000.

Makinson, Larry.
***Speaking Freely: Washington
Insiders Talk About Money
in Politics.***
Washington, D.C.: Center for
Responsive Politics, 2003 (2nd ed.).

Smith, Hedrick.
***The Power Game: How
Washington Works.***
New York: Ballantine Books, 1989.

## INTERNET SITES

**CNN.com—Inside Politics**
http://www.cnn.com/ALLPOLITICS/
Popular site for political news.

**C-SPAN**
http://www.c-span.org/
Cable network that covers Congress.

**Democratic National Committee**
http://www.democrats.org/
Official Democratic Party site.

**Federal Election Commission**
http://www.fec.gov/
Official site of the FEC.

**GOP.com—Republican National
Committee**
http://www.gop.com/
Official Republican Party site.

**Opensecrets.org**
http://www.opensecrets.org/
Shows where senators and representatives get their campaign cash.

# INDEX

Page numbers in *italic* type refer to illustration captions.

# INDEX (CONT.)